ART FOR YOUNG PEOPLE

Claude
Monet

Important events in the life of

Claude Monet

1840   Born in Paris on November 14.

1845   Family moves to Le Havre, where his father runs a grocery business.

1857   His mother dies.

1856–59 Sells caricatures in Le Havre and first meets Boudin.

1859   Despite his father's opposition, goes to Paris to study as an artist. Enrolls at the Académie Suisse.

1861   Conscripted into the army. Catches typhoid fever and is sent home.

1862   Convalesces in Le Havre, painting with Boudin and Jongkind. Returns to Paris and enrolls at Gleyre's studio, where his fellow students are Renoir, Bazille and Sisley.

1865–66 Three paintings are accepted for exhibition at the Paris Salon.

1869   Paints with Renoir at La Grenouillère near Paris.

1870   Marries Camille Doncieux. Prussian army advances on Paris. Monet flees to London.

1874   First Impressionist exhibition. His painting *Impression: Sunrise* gives rise to the name Impressionism.

1879   Camille dies.

1890   Buys a house at Giverny.

1892   Marries Alice Hoschedé.

1908   Eyesight starts to fail.

1911   Alice dies.

1918   Begins the water-lily project.

1926   Dies at Giverny December 5.

Claude Monet

Peter
Harrison

Claude Monet, Renoir, 1875

STERLING PUBLISHING CO., INC.   NEW YORK

Impression: Sunrise, 1872

This painting by Monet was first shown at an exhibition in 1874. The exhibition showed work by Monet and his group of friends. Because their style of painting was very different from traditional painting, many people were shocked. The group was nicknamed "the Impressionists"—a name taken from the title of the painting above. Today their style of painting is known as Impressionism and their work is much admired.

Cover: *Rue Saint-Denis, Fête du 30 Juin 1878*

End paper: detail from *The Water-Lilies: Green Reflections* (right)

Paintings in this book are identified by their title followed by the artist who painted them. If no artist is named the painting is by Monet.

This book was prepared for Macdonald Young Books Ltd by Globe Education of Nantwich, Cheshire

Design concept by M&M Design Partnership

Artwork by Edward Lightfoot

Subject Adviser Professor Arthur Hughes Department of Art, University of Central England, Birmingham

French Adviser Sophie Charpentier

Library of Congress Cataloging-in-Publication Data Available

10 9 8 7 6 5 4 3 2 1

Published 1996 by Sterling Publishing Company Inc. 387 Park Avenue South, New York, NY 10016
Originally published in Great Britain by Macdonald Young Books Ltd under the title *An Introduction to Claude Monet*
© 1995 by Globe education
Distributed in Canada by Sterling Publishing c/o Canadian Manda Group, One Atlantic Avenue, Suite 105 Toronto, Ontario, Canada M6K 3E7
Printed and bound in Portugal
All rights reserved

Sterling ISBN 0-8069-6158-9

Acknowledgments

The Art Institute Chicago 7 photograph © 1995, The Art Institute, Chicago
Bibliothèque Nationale 9b, 15b
Bridgeman Art Library, London: cover, Musée des Beaux Arts, Rouen/Lauros/Giraudon; end paper,

Musée de l'Orangerie, Paris/Lauros/Giraudon; title page Musée d'Orsay, Paris; 4, Musée Marmottan, Paris; 6, Christie's London; 7t, Agnew & Sons, London; 10t Kunsthalle, Bremen/Lauros-Giraudon; 10b, Metropolitan Museum of Art, New York; 11, Puskin Museum, Moscow; 12, National Gallery, London; 13t, Musée de la Ville de Paris, Musée Carnavalet/Giraudon; 13b, Christie's London; 14, National Gallery, London; 15t, Musée de la Ville de Paris, Musée Carnavalet/Giraudon; 22, Hermitage, St Petersburg; 23b, Musée d'Orsay, Paris; 25, National Gallery, London; 29, Musée de l'Orangerie, Paris/Lauros-Giraudon
British Museum, 21b
Heather Angel 26, 27
The National Gallery, London 8, 13t
Reproduced with the permission of the Trustees
Roger Viollet 28
Tate Gallery, London 23t
Tony Stone 24

Contents

A busy port

Claude Monet was born in 1840 in Paris, the capital city of France. He was almost 5 years old when his family moved to Le Havre, which is a port on the French coast to the northwest of Paris. Here Claude grew up with the smell of the sea and the sights and sounds of the port.

He hated school but liked painting and drawing. By the time he was 14 years old he was quite skillful and often made funny drawings of people he knew.

▲ **Places that Monet Knew**
This map shows the main places in France where Monet lived and painted. They were mostly close to the River Seine, which flows through Paris to the sea at Le Havre.

◄ **The Jetty at Trouville, Bodin, 1888**
Eugène Boudin liked to paint outside. Sometimes he took young Monet with him.

■ *The blue-gray of the sea and the sky cover most of the picture. Boudin used patches of bright colors to pick out the people on the jetty, for the boats and their sails.*

Monet was still a schoolboy selling his drawings at an art shop when he first met the painter Eugène Boudin.

Boudin often went on trips to paint the scenery along the coast near Le Havre. He was much older than Monet but grew to like the young boy and invited him to go painting with him.

For Monet painting alongside an artist in the open air was an exciting new experience that changed his life. Later, Monet was to talk about this time and say, "My eyes were opened."

Monet's Drawings ▲
Monet's first drawings were portraits of people he knew. They usually had large heads and funny faces. Drawings like this are called caricatures.

Lightweight Easels ▼
In the 1840s, artists could buy lightweight painting equipment for the first time. This meant they could go out and paint in the open air. Before this, they could only make sketches of outdoor scenes and had to work on their paintings in their studios.

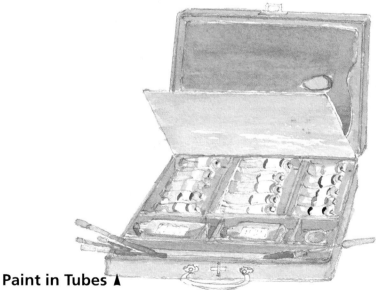

Paint in Tubes ▲
In the 1840s, good-quality paint in tubes was on sale in shops. Artists no longer needed to make their own paints by grinding colored pigments into oils.

The painter's life

Monet first went to Paris to study art in 1859. Many artists lived and worked in Paris and Monet knew he could learn from them. He joined an art class, visited exhibitions of paintings and became friendly with several other young painters. But his life changed suddenly when he was forced to join the French army.

He was sent to Algeria in North Africa. He did not mind army life too much, but he really wanted to be a painter.

After two years, Monet became ill and was allowed to go home to Le Havre. Through his friend Boudin, he met a Dutch painter, Johan Jongkind. Jongkind, who was much older than Monet, specialized in painting sea scenes. Like Boudin, Jongkind tried to paint directly from nature. He often painted pictures of the coast in watercolor and then, back in his studio, used them to create oil paintings of the same scenes.

◄ **The Museum at Le Havre, 1873**
Monet often painted the scenes around his home in Le Havre. This view of the harbor shows sailing boats in front of the museum, which was bombed in World War II.

■ *The smoothness of the ships's sails contrast with the roughness of the stone walls of the museum behind. The flecks of which paint on the water make the surface of the sea look as though it is moving.*

Large Sailing Boats at Honfleur ➤
Johan Jongkind, 1865
Jongkind's knowledge of Dutch painting made him work hard at showing the effects of light in his own pictures. Monet said later in his life "… Jongkind was my true master."

Jongkind used quick, rough brush strokes when painting, which helped him to show the effect of light flickering on water. His pictures are not careful copies of a scene but make you feel what it would be like to be there. This was what Monet liked about his work.

Monet admired Jongkind's work and learned from him how to look at a scene and pick out the important features. Jongkind was so important to Monet that he once said "Jongkind was my true master."

Monet as a young man ➤
Monet was a rather handsome young man, very confident and determined to succeed in his chosen career as an artist.

When he had recovered his health, Monet returned to Paris, where he enrolled at another studio. He became firm friends with other students, especially Frédéric Bazille, Alfred Sisley and Auguste Renoir. He went with his new friends on painting drips in the open air. They found landscapes to paint near Paris, in the forests around the village of Chailly, close to Fontainebleau castle.

9

First success

▲ The Woman in the Green Dress, 1866
This life-size painting was shown at the 1866 Salon. The model was Camille Doncieux, whom Monet later married.

Every year in Paris, there was a large art exhibition called the Salon. Young artists wanted to show their paintings at this exhibition but first the paintings had to be accepted by the judges. Some painters tried many times to have their work accepted, but without success.

Monet was very talented and had two paintings accepted the first year he put forward any of his work. People who visited the 1865 Salon thought he was a promising young artist.

◄ The Terrace at Sainte-Adresse, 1867
This painting shows the terrace at the Monet home in Le Havre. The man wearing a straw hat and sitting at the front is Monet's father.

■ *Most French paintings of people in the nineteenth century showed them indoors. Monet tried to find new ways to show people in the open air on bright, sunny days.*

▲ The Picnic, 1866
It was not usual for artists to paint such large paintings of ordinary people. This is the middle part of the painting. It measures 98 by 85 inches. Camille Doncieux, Monet's girl friend, was the model for all the women in the picture.

■ *Monet used patches of bright color to show the effect of the sunlight through the trees. You can see these patches on the tablecloth and on the seated woman's dress. Other less bright patches are on the heads, arms and shoulders of the other people.*

Monet was thrilled to have his paintings shown at the Salon and started a grand new painting that he wanted to enter for the exhibition the next year. It was a huge picture showing 12 people enjoying a picnic on the grass, surrounded by trees.

The picture measured nearly 20 by 13 feet and Monet worked very hard. But it was not finished before the last entry date for the exhibition and he gave up. Later, the painting was cut up into three pieces. Only two of these pieces still exist.

Holidays

In the summer, people living in Paris liked to escape from the hot city. For short breaks, they went to small towns and villages on the outskirts of Paris. When they had more time, they often traveled to the coast near Le Havre.

Along the River Seine, small cafés and restaurants opened for the visitors from Paris. There were musicians who played and sang while the holiday-makers swam in the river, went boating and enjoyed eating.

When Monet lived in Paris, many of his favorite painting spots were just outside the city. He liked the views of the River Seine and the woods around Fontainebleau.

He was very poor at this time. Despite his early success, the paintings he entered for the 1867 and 1869 Salons were rejected by the judges.

◄ **The Beach at Trouville, 1870**
Trouville was a popular holiday resort near Le Havre. People sat on the beach in their ordinary clothes. Sunbathing was unknown and women shaded their faces from the sun.

■ *Monet painted this scene in a new and daring way. Strong colors and patches of bright white show the effect of the sunlight on the women, on their clothes and on the beach.*

Le Grenouillère, 1869, Monet and Renoir ➤
Monet and his painter friends went on painting trips together. Renoir (left) and Monet (right) both painted the same café at a swimming place on the River Seine.

Monet painted at great speed with bright dashes of color. His scene is alive with light, activity and bustle. Renoir painted with light feathery brush strokes. He wanted to show what the people were like.

Paris ▼
Paris in the nineteenth century was an important meeting point for people from many countries.

The Universal ▲ **Exhibition, Paris, 1889**

The Boulevard des Italiens, Paris, Grandjean, 1889 ➤

In 1870, the Salon again rejected the paintings that Monet entered. One of them was his painting of the bathers at La Grenouillère on the River Seine. Today, people believe this painting was an important turning point in Monet's experiments. They look on it as the first Impressionist painting.

Charles-François Daubigny, a landscape painter, admired Monet's work. He was one of the judges for the Salon and resigned from the Salon jury in 1870 because they would not exhibit any of Monet's paintings that year.

13

London and back

Monet and his friends lived in France at a time when it was a large, growing nation. In 1870, France declared war against Prussia, a country to the east. France and Prussia were arguing over who should be the next king of Spain.

For ordinary people, the war meant hunger, injury or death. Many Frenchmen were forced into the army.

One of Monet's painter friends, Bazille, did join the army and was killed in a battle in November.

By now Monet had a wife and child. If he died fighting, there would be nobody to look after them. He decided to move to London until the war was over.

View of the Thames, 1871 ▼
Monet visited England several times. He did many paintings of the River Thames.

Parisians queuing at the door of a grocery store in 1870, when Paris was surrounded by Prussian troops.

Monet went to London with a letter to introduce him to a French art dealer who lived there. Monet hoped to sell him some paintings. The dealer was Paul Durand-Ruel. Later, he would become one of the most important dealers in Monet's work.

The letter of introduction contained the words "*Buy his work.*" It was written by François Daubigny, the painter who had resigned from the Salon because they would not show Monet's work.

The French made peace with the Prussians in 1871. Monet returned to France in October and rented a house at Argenteuil near Paris.

The End of the War ▼
The people of Paris tore down a statue of the French Emperor because they were angry that the Prussians had won the war.

15

Family life

Monet had many friends, but his family was at the center of his life. When he was young, his parents and, most of all, his aunt, Marie-Jeanne Lecadre, gave him the help he needed to become an artist. Often during his long life, he went back to the town of Le Havre, where he grew up. He often painted the coast he knew so well.

When he went to Paris, he met Camille Doncieux. They stayed together throughout his many moves and, in 1871, they went to live in Argenteuil, which was to be their home for 9 years. Camille and their first son, Jean, often appear in Monet's paintings of the 1870s, usually in sunlit views of the garden at Argenteuil or walking in the nearby countryside.

THE MONET FAMILY

Claude Monet married *Camille Doncieux*
born 1840 1870 born 1847
died 1926 died 1879

Jean *Michel*
born 1867 born 1878
died 1914 died 1966

▲ **The Monet Family**
Claude Monet married Camille Doncieux in 1870. They had two sons, Jean, the elder son, married Blanche Hoschedé but was killed in action during World War I. The younger son, Michel, inherited Giverny when his father died in 1926.

◄ **Monet Family in the Garden, Manet, 1874**
Édouard Manet, an artist friend, often visited the Monet family. In this painting he shows Camille and Jean sitting together beneath a tree with Claude Monet gardening in the background.

The Kitchen at Giverny ►
Monet's house and garden at
Giverny are now a museum.
Some rooms are kept
as they were during
Monet's lifetime, when
the blue kitchen,
shown here, was
the center of
the household.

Monet was employed
to paint for Ernest
Hoschedé, a rich
businessman who
owned a chateau near
Monet's home. But Ernest lost
most of his money. The chateau
was sold and his wife, Alice, and
their children moved in with the
Monets.

Michel Monet was born in 1878
and a year later Camille died.
Alice Hoschedé then took care of
Camille's children as well as her
own and helped Monet to bring up
his two sons.

Over time, they became one large family and
lived first at Vétheuil and later at Giverny.
In 1892, after Ernest died, Monet and Alice
were able to marry. They lived happily
together for another 19 years, until Alice's
death in 1911. Her daughter Blanche then
cared for Monet until
the end of
his life.

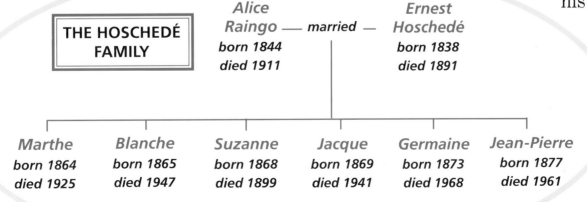

THE HOSCHEDÉ FAMILY

Alice Raingo — married — *Ernest Hoschedé*
born 1844 *born 1838*
died 1911 *died 1891*

Marthe	*Blanche*	*Suzanne*	*Jacque*	*Germaine*	*Jean-Pierre*
born 1864	*born 1865*	*born 1868*	*born 1869*	*born 1873*	*born 1877*
died 1925	*died 1947*	*died 1899*	*died 1941*	*died 1968*	*died 1961*

Iron and steam

The railway network in France is world famous. It carries people and goods very quickly to all parts of the country. In Monet's lifetime, it was a new invention. Railway tracks were built between the main cities and engines were built with huge boilers that made steam to drive the wheels and pull the carriages.

Monet loved to paint these new machines surrounded by steam at a station or with long trails of smoke behind them. He was fascinated by the way the light was changed by the billows of steam and smoke.

▲ **The Gare de l'Est, Paris**

Many of Monet's train paintings were done while he lived at Argenteuil. There was a new railway bridge over the River Seine nearby that he loved to paint usually with a train crossing.

He also painted a whole series of trains in a station in Paris known at the Gare Saint-Lazare. He rented a room near the station and used it as a studio. It is said that the station master kept engines standing on the tracks so that Monet could finish his paintings.

French locomotives ▼

As the railway system spread out across France, workshops were busy making more engines. Engines had a boiler and a tender to carry coal. One man drove the train and another stoked the fire with coal so that there was always plenty of steam.

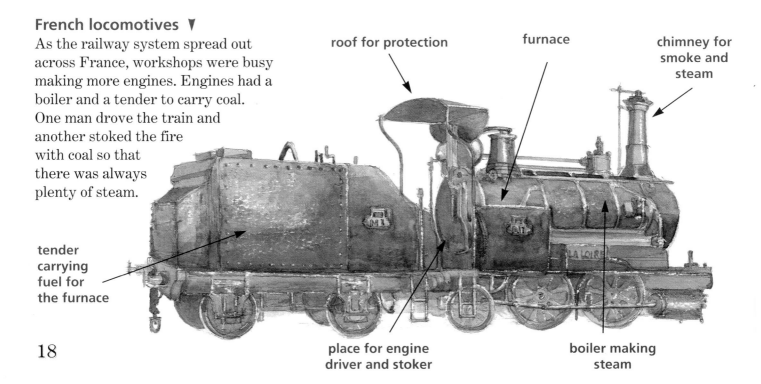

roof for protection

furnace

chimney for smoke and steam

tender carrying fuel for the furnace

place for engine driver and stoker

boiler making steam

The Gare Saint-Lazare was a wonderful new building in Monet's time. It had iron girders and huge sheets of glass for the roof and was quite different from the buildings people were used to. It was the terminus for trains from the north of Paris and is still a main railway station today.

◼ *Monet used the strong lines made by the girders holding the roof of the station to form a frame for the top of the painting.*

The railway tracks at the bottom of the painting and the platforms on the left and right lead your eye straight to the trains that are just coming into the station.

◼ ▲ **The Gare Saint-Lazare, 1877**
Monet made many sketches of the station and produced a series of 12 paintings. Sometimes he sat painting at his easel outside on the tracks. The station was very busy and it is likely that he had to finish some of the paintings in his studio.

◼ *Monet loved the steam given off by the trains. He used wispy brush strokes of white paint to show it billowing around the station. Darker blue paint shows the smoke coming out of the train's chimney.*

Living by water

Growing up by the sea, Monet was used to seeing the sea and sky in many moods. Sometimes it would be still and calm but at other times stormy with dark clouds, strong winds and crashing waves. His first painting teachers, Boudin and Jongkind, showed him how to make paintings out of the scenes he saw along the coast.

Throughout his life Monet was fascinated by painting water. His paintings show the sea and the River Seine in many ways. In his later years he painted numerous pictures of the lily pond in his garden at Giverny.

Monet owned four boats during his life. They were small vessels for sailing on the river. The most important to him was his floating studio.

The idea for the floating studio came from Monet's old friend François Daubigny. It was an ordinary boat with a small cabin on top. Painting in a boat gave a better view of the river. The artist could choose where to paint and could sit in the boat while it was raining. He could also keep canvasses and other painting equipment in the boat, ready for when he needed them.

The Studio Boat ▼

canopy to keep out sun and rain

deck with enough space to sit and paint

cabin to store canvasses and painting equipment

◄ **The Boat at Giverny**
Monet had all four of his boats at Giverny when he moved there in 1883. This painting shows Alice Hoschedé's daughters fishing on the River Epte. Germaine is standing in the prow, Suzanne is sitting in the middle and Blanche is in the sterm.

■ *The girls and the inside of the boat are painted in pale colors so that they stand out against the deep green of the river. Their reflections help to give depth to the water.*

Japanese Art ►
Monet had a deep interest in Japanese art. His ideas for boats were perhaps based on Japanese prints like this one.

Argenteuil was a favorite place for the people who lived in Paris. Some of them kept small yachts on the river there. On summer weekends they would spend their days on the water and sometimes held yacht races. Monet loved being surrounded by crowds of small boats, and they were the subject of many of his paintings while he lived there.

"I will yet make progress"

As the day goes from sunrise to sunset, the color and strength of the light changes. A tree seen on a summer morning can look very different by the time evening comes. The position of the sun has changed and the colors and the shadows are different. Also, the same tree looks very different in winter.

Monet's greatest interest was to paint these changes. In his early years, he often became cross because changes in the weather could stop him from painting for days on end. Suppose he started a painting on a dull day.

Then suppose the weather became sunny. He would have to wait until the weather became dull again before he could get on with his picture.

Finally, Monet had the idea of taking several canvasses with him when he went out painting. If the day started dull, he would paint the dull picture. If it then turned sunny, he would change canvasses and paint the sunny picture. When it came to late afternoon, he would paint the late afternoon picture. This way he built up whole series of pictures showing the same object at different times of day and year.

◄ **Haystack, 1890–91**
Monet chose to paint the haystacks in a field near his house. Haystacks were a good choice because they stay in the same place for a long period of time.

In total he made 15 paintings showing the stacks in winter, spring, summer and at different times of day. This one shows a haystack at evening in early summer.

Poplars on the Epte, 1891 ►

Monet painted this group of poplar trees by the River Epte from his floating studio. He bought the land to prevent anyone from cutting the poplars down while he was painting them. There were 20 pictures in all.

Cathedral at Rouen: Harmony in Blue and Gold, Full Sunlight 1894 ▼

The painting below shows one of the many views Monet painted of Rouen Cathedral in 1892 and 1893. As the sun rose in the east in the morning and sank in the west in the afternoon, the shadows on the stone changed, making the color of the cathedral look different at different times of day. Monet tried to capture these changes in his series of paintings of the cathedral.

■ *On the left of the picture the Albane Tower reaches up to the sky. Its top is cut off by the painting's edge. The roof of the nave (the main part of the cathedral) is drenched in sunshine.*

■ *There are many carvings on the front of the nave. The walls are thick, and deep shadows form in the windows and doors. Monet manages to show this massive structure using patches of color.*

23

"Giverny is splendid"

In 1883, Monet moved his family to Giverny, a village northwest of Paris. The house at Giverny was to be his home until he died 37 years later. It was a long building, painted pink on the outside and two stories high. It was big enough to take Monet's large family in comfort.

While Monet lived at Argenteuil, he had become an enthusiastic gardener and had a great interest in different kinds of plants and flowers. The house at Giverny had a very large garden and Monet soon set about rearranging it.

▲ **The House at Giverny**
This was a comfortable family home surrounded by a large garden. At first, Monet rented, but later he could afford to buy it.

◄ **The Yellow Dining Room**
The dining room at Giverny is kept as it was in Monet's time. Here the family would eat lunch at midday and supper at about 7:30 in the evening.

The Water-Lily Pond and the Japanese Bridge, 1899 ►

Monet built a Japanese bridge over the small lake in his garden. He planted wisteria to grow over the bridge and water lilies in the lake. In 1899, he began a series of paintings of the bridge. This painting shows the bridge on a summer afternoon.

The first thing you see in this picture is the strong curve of the bridge and this leads you to look at the water lilies below. Monet left out the sky on purpose, because it would take your eye away from the bridge and the pond.

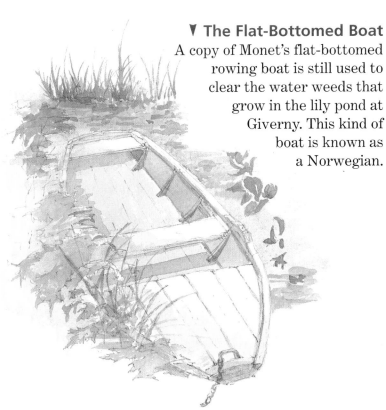

▼ The Flat-Bottomed Boat
A copy of Monet's flat-bottomed rowing boat is still used to clear the water weeds that grow in the lily pond at Giverny. This kind of boat is known as a Norwegian.

The household was organized around Monet's needs. He got up early in the morning, had a cold bath and breakfast. Then he went out to paint until lunchtime and went out painting again in the afternoon until supper time. He usually went to bed at 9:30 pm so that he could get up early the next day.

The children often went out with him and helped to carry his canvasses, easel and paints. If the weather was wet, Monet was very bad-tempered and sometimes stayed in bed all day.

25

Gardens and flowers

The gardens that Monet made at Giverny are now almost as famous as his paintings. Visitors travel from all over the world to see them.

Soon after renting "the pink house" Monet found a swampy hollow on the other side of the railway line at the end of the garden. He heard that the local town council were going to drain it and so he bought it to make a pond there. Over the years, he surrounded the pond with trees and flowers and grew water lilies in it. It became known as "the water garden."

Japanese Anemones ➤
Monet planted many plants from Eastern Asia in his garden. Their pink and white blooms made the kind of color effects he liked to paint.

To look after the main garden, Monet had a full-time gardener and four part-time assistants. He bullied them, arguing about which flowers should go where and how best they should be looked after. He cared just as much about his gardens as he did about his paintings, and spent much of his spare time walking around them inspecting the plants.

Bamboo ➤
Bamboo grew originally in China and Japan, though it is now very common in Europe.

The Style of the Gardens at Giverny

Monet did not try to make a neat garden where the plants grew in rows. He liked plants to grow over the edges of the paths and flower beds as they would in nature. He was very careful about the colors and textures of the plants that grew next to one another.

▼ **Wisteria**

Key
1. The house
2. Studios
3. Japanese anemones
4. The Japanese bridge with wisteria growing over it
5. The water lily pond
6. Bamboo

Water Lilies ▲

"I have work to do"

When Alice died in 1911, Monet was overcome with despair. For the second time in his life, he had lost a much-loved wife. Friends worried that he might never paint again. Slowly, however, he came to terms with his sadness and began work on his last and greatest project.

This was "the water lilies," a series of huge paintings of the lilies that floated in the water garden at Giverny. Monet had agreed with the French Government that he would give the paintings to the French Nation. They now hang in two very large, oval rooms in the Orangerie Museum in Paris.

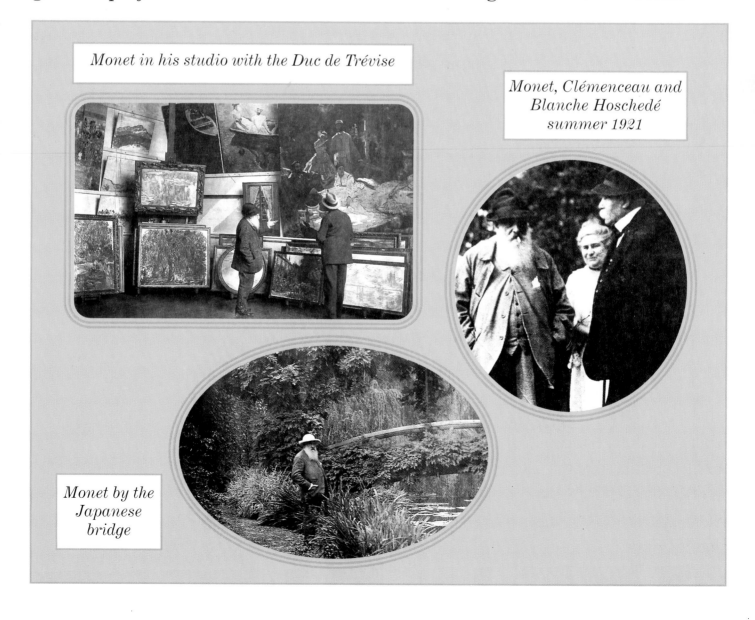

Monet in his studio with the Duc de Trévise

Monet, Clémenceau and Blanche Hoschedé summer 1921

Monet by the Japanese bridge

Monet kept paintings from all periods of his life around him. As he grew older, more and more people came to visit him and pay their respects to the greatest living French painter. He showed them around his studio and his garden and talked to them about his work.

In the last years of his life, Monet was worried about going blind. He was in his eightieth year and his eyesight was failing. Growths called cataracts were making it more difficult for him to see clearly.

▲ **The Water Lilies**
The paintings were hung in two enormous oval rooms that were built specially to house them. They stretch all the way around the rooms, making visitors feel as though they are part of the water lilies on the pond. The painting above is from the picture known as "Green Reflections."

In 1923, an operation to remove the cataracts gave Monet some of his sight back. He was able to continue working to finish the water lily project.

Monet died at Giverny on December 5, 1926, and the water lilies were installed in the Orangerie the following year.

More information

Glossary

canvas Woven cloth on which artists make their oil paintings. The cloth must first be sealed with a coating known as a ground and stretched on a frame.

caricature A way of drawing people in which their features are distorted or exaggerated.

cataract A condition of the eye in which the lens becomes more and more opaque.

Impressionism A style of painting that developed in France around 1860 that tried to show an immediate visual impression of a scene. It involved new techniques and new choices of subjects. Many people were shocked, but it has become one of the most important changes in art of the 19th and 20th centuries.

Impressionists The first Impressionist artists were Monet, Renoire, Sisley and Bazille. They soon included Pissarro, Cézanne, Morisot and Guillaumin, and later Degas and Manet. There were eight exhibitions of the work between 1874 and 1886.

oil paint The most usual painting material used by European artists since the 16th century. It consists of colored substances called pigments mixed with oil. The oil is usually linseed or walnut oil. In the 1850s paint became available in collapsible tin tubes, but until then artists needed to make their own paints by grinding pigments into oil—a slow and difficult process.

Prussia A German kingdom that became important in the 18th century. In 1870 France and Prussia were at war.

pigment A colored substance that can be ground to a fine dust and mixed with oil to form paint. Most pigments today are synthetic, but earlier they came from a variety of mineral, plant and animal sources.

The Salon The annual exhibition of the French Royal Academy of Painting and Sculpture. It was first held in 1667.

water-color Paint that can be thinned with water.

World War I A war fought between 1914 and 1918 mostly in Europe.

World War II A war fought between 1939 and 1945 in Europe, Africa and Asia.

People

Frédéric Bazille (1841–70) French painter, one of the first Impressionists, died during the Prussian War fighting for France.

Eugène Boudin (1824–98) French painter of beach scenes and seascapes. He liked to paint in the open air.

Charles-François Daubigny (1817–78) French landscape painter, one of the first painters to work in the open air.

Paul Durand-Ruel (1831–1922) French art dealer who supported the Impressionists and was the first dealer to sell their work.

Johan Barthold Jongkind (1819–91) Dutch landscape painter who made drawings and watercolor sketches in the open air and used them to make oil paintings in his studio.

Édouard Manet (1832–83) French painter and graphic artist. An associate of the Impressionists, he is seen as one of the founders of modern art.

Pierre-Auguste Renoir (1841–1919) French Impressionist painter.

Alfred Sisley (1839–99) French Impressionist painter who had English parents but mostly lived and worked in Paris.

Index